ADVANCE PRAISE

I have been a Michelle Dobbins fan for a long time. I'm so glad she has graced the world with a missing piece of the puzzle. Law of Attraction works when our joy channels are open. Thanks, Michelle, for reminding us.

~Pam Grout
author of E-Squared, E-Cubed, and 15 other books
www.pamgrout.com

Michelle is not just a gifted writer, she's also the real deal when it comes to conscious creation. Her Personal Alchemy program is engaging, inspiring and fun to boot. Time in Michelle's world is time well spent!

~Jeannette Maw
The Good Vibe Coach & founder of Good Vibe University
www.goodvibeblog.com

In *Personal Alchemy*, Michelle Dobbins makes the art of manifestation approachable and fun. Filled with exercises we can do to raise our energy vibrations, *Personal Alchemy* can be used as a powerful tool to align ourselves with the life we desire. If you are confused about how to apply the Law of Attraction, and are ready to experience a life full of miracles, you must read this book.

~Cloris Kylie
author of Magnificent... Married or Not
www.cloriskylie.com

This super short, crystal clear book shines like a beacon from amongst the plethora of books about how to have a happy life. Michelle Martin Dobbins explores how each person has the power to use their 'personal alchemy' - not in order to make things happen; but in order to reconnect with our true, powerful selves. This is much more than some formulaic "do this and you'll be happy" set of instructions. In fact, Dobbins takes the whole "Law of Attraction" concept, picks it apart, shakes it up, gives it a thorough overhaul, adds in all the missing pieces - and finally puts it back together into a far broader, more inclusive and more powerful approach. Powerful, yes, but also eminently simple and do-able. This is also an entertaining read, with notes of humor, plenty of honesty about the author's own journey, and impeccable references. The kind of book I'll be keeping on my bedside for daily reference: highly recommended for veterans of deliberate creation and newbies alike. Alchemy, activate!

~Janette Dalgliesh
Brain Whisperer
http://www.youreverydaysuperpower.com

PERSONAL
Alchemy

PERSONAL
Alchemy

The Missing Ingredient for Law of Attraction Success

MICHELLE MARTIN DOBBINS

ISBN 13: 978-1-942430-85-8
ISBN 10: 1-942430-85-X

Year of the Book
135 Glen Avenue
Glen Rock, PA 17327

Front Cover Design: John Matthews

DEDICATION

To my husband, David and my children:
Serenity, Kadin, Kali and Violet.

Thanks for being the individuals that you are.
My life is infinitely fuller and richer because of you.
You are a dream I didn't remember dreaming
until you came true.

TABLE OF CONTENTS

Chapter One:

The Law of Attraction is Missing an Ingredient

Dear Michelle,

I need some help with the Law of Attraction - it doesn't work for me. I make vision boards and put them on my bedroom wall, even though my husband laughs at them. I say affirmations every morning and night and nothing changes. My husband still smokes pot every day and I'm pretty sure he's having an affair.

My kids don't listen to me and I feel like a failure as a mom. My teenage son skips school all the time and I think he might be doing drugs (although since his father does drugs, it makes it hard for me to say much). My daughter is only eight, but she acts like she hates me and she struggles in school. I'm afraid she is not going to pass the second grade.

My boss is always on my case and I hate my job. Maybe if we got a new manager things would get better here, but he always yells at everyone and he has no management skills. I just don't understand why everyone else talks about how the law of attraction gets them everything they want. I do all the techniques every day and my life still sucks. All I want is a better job, a better marriage and better kids. Is that too much to ask? Why doesn't it work for me? Please help!

—Lost in Louisville

Okay, that's not a real letter, but I get emails and messages similar to this every week. This is just a compilation of the most common problems people share with me. It's a reflection of the many messages I've received in the past year.

I'm not making fun of anyone, because I know their pain is real. I've been the person who was struggling to find happiness and felt like it was going to elude me my whole life. Anyone who feels like the Law of Attraction doesn't work for them can breathe sigh of relief now – you're in good company.

In this book, I'm going to tell you why it doesn't always work and what's missing that keeps it from working. You will then know how to change your life and make your dreams come true.

My blog, Daily Alchemy, won best Law of Attraction blog from LOA Leaders in 2012 and 2013, and I'm super proud of that fact. Some of my favorite people are law of attraction coaches. Though I tag almost every blog post with the terms "law of attraction" (and it's shorthand "LOA"), there's a reason my blog is called Daily Alchemy and not Daily LOA – it may come as a bit of a surprise that I hate the words "law of attraction." Don't get me wrong, we create our own reality, but I'm not sure that the law of attraction alone is always the best or most effective way to deliberately do it.

I don't hate the law of attraction – I hate the term. The words "law of attraction" makes me cringe for two reasons. One, "law of attraction" has become a "buzz phrase" that encompasses so many things. Like any other movement there are wonderful and fabulous people associated with it and, unfortunately, some that are not so fabulous and wonderful. Many people don't really understand LOA, and they end up disheartened when it doesn't seem to work for them.

The other reason is that, as many others have said, it's just one law of our universe. Does it even seem to make sense that we would live in a universe as complex and beautiful as this that is governed by just one law? There are many laws we can use to create our best lives, and the law of attraction is certainly a wonderful one, but there are others that define and regulate our creative force as well.

If the law of attraction is the only tool you use, you may miss out on a lot of the richness and deeper significance of creating your own reality.

What Is The Law Of Attraction?

Esther Hicks, who channels Abraham – a collective nonphysical energy – first popularized this term. I enjoy most of their work and their explanations for how best to use the law of attraction, but many times their statements have either been misunderstood or taken out of context. Here is their definition of the Universal Law of Attraction:

> *Everything in your life and the lives of those around you is affected by the Law of Attraction. It is the basis of everything that comes into your experience. An awareness of the Law of Attraction and an understanding of how it works is essential*

to living life on purpose. In fact, it is essential to living the life of joy that you came forth to live.

The Law of Attraction says: That which is like unto itself, is drawn. When you say, "Birds of a feather flock together," you are actually talking about the Law of Attraction. You see the Law of Attraction evidenced in your society when you see that the one who speaks most about illness has illness; when you see that the one who speaks most about prosperity has prosperity.

As you begin to understand – or better stated, as you begin to remember – this powerful Law of Attraction, the evidence of it that surrounds you will be easily apparent, for you will begin to recognize the exact correlation between what you have been thinking about and what is actually coming into your experience. Nothing merely shows up in your experience. You attract it – all of it. No exceptions.

—*Abraham-Hicks*

This definition is good, but some of the references can be misunderstood. It takes more than thinking or speaking about a topic to attract it as a lasting change in your life. Many people think about money all day and wonder why they don't attract it, but they don't realize they are worrying about not having it instead of actually appreciating and enjoying the money they already have.

Many people become frightened by their own negative thoughts and feelings and try to hide them because they worry that the law of attraction will "bite" them if they think negatively.

Abraham tells us to aim for 51% positive thoughts and it will be plenty to change our lives, but a lot of people miss that part of the teaching and create more problems by beating themselves up for thinking negatively.

The Urban Dictionary defines law of attraction this way:

> *The belief that positive thoughts are magnets for positive life experiences and negative thoughts are magnets for negative life experiences.* ***Based on the law of attraction, if you have a specific desire and focus joyfully on that desire, it will be fulfilled.***
>
> —*Abraham720 on Urban Dictionary*

This definition focuses too much on thought, but I like the addition of the word joyfully, because the way we feel about our thoughts makes a big difference in our results.

Here is what Wikipedia had as a definition to the law of attraction:

> *The **law of attraction** is the name given to the belief that "like attracts like" and that by focusing on positive or negative thoughts, one can bring about positive or negative results. This belief is based upon the idea that people and their thoughts are both made from pure energy, and the belief that like energy attracts like energy. One example used*

by a proponent of the law of attraction is that if a person opened an envelope expecting to see a bill, then the law of attraction would "confirm" those thoughts and contain a bill when opened. A person who decided to instead expect a cheque might, under the same law, find a cheque instead of a bill. Although there are some cases where positive or negative attitudes can produce corresponding results (principally the placebo and nocebo effects), there is no scientific basis to the law of attraction.

It's obvious that whoever wrote this definition does not believe in the law of attraction, and they have oversimplified it. It's this kind of oversimplification which causes a lot of people to think it "doesn't work" for them. What I really love about this definition is that it states "like energy attracts like energy." This gets closer to what we need to believe, rather than just thinking our thoughts attract what we want. Our thoughts create our feelings, and our feelings create our vibrations, or who we are at that moment. Who we are at this moment in time is the place we are attracting from.

The law of attraction always exists. It is not something you decide to practice any more than you decide to practice the law of gravity – it simply is. Though you can't actively practice it in that sense, you can learn techniques to work with it in a way that is helpful to you.

My quick definition of the law of attraction is "you get what you are." Notice I did not say you get what you put on a vision board, what you affirm or what you pray or journal about. All law of attraction techniques are meant to shift your vibration so that you become a match to what you want, and what you want becomes attracted to you.

Some Common Misconceptions About The Law Of Attraction

I cringe when someone asks me if the law of attraction really works, because I know I can't give them an easy answer. I must first explain what it is, then how to work with it for the best results. Lots of people have many misconceptions about what the law of attraction is and how it works. Here are a few that I see over and over:

MISCONCEPTION

If I keep saying this Affirmation over and over, eventually it will happen.

This isn't true unless saying the affirmation creates a change in how you feel – that is how you can tell when an affirmation is helpful. If it succeeds in changing how you feel, it's one that is likely to "work." If you feel joy when you say it, it's perfect. If you feel anxious, bored, or disbelief, you need to change your affirmation until the feelings you experience are positive. Affirmations are a tool to help you shift your vibration, and your vibration is what attracts what you want – not the affirmation itself.

MISCONCEPTION

*If I think a negative thought,
everything is going to go horribly wrong.*

One negative thought is not going to create bad things in your life. Of course, the more positive your thoughts and the more you focus on what's going right, the higher your vibration is going to be, but you don't need to run from negative thoughts. That's probably the worst thing to do. If you find it easy to shift to a positive thought, then by all means, do it. The problem is that many people cover up negative or painful feelings and pretend they don't exist. It won't work in the long run. Your vibration doesn't lie. If you are pretending to be happy, but have a lot of feelings you haven't dealt with under that pretension, you won't have good results from law of attraction techniques. I've found the best thing to do is just sit down and honor your feelings. Let it be okay to feel how you feel, for as long as you need to – just stop telling the story about it. Once you feel the feeling without the story, the feeling goes away pretty quickly and your vibration will rise.

MISCONCEPTION

It's my fault that I'm sick.

We need to take responsibility for our lives, but beating ourselves up because we attracted something we don't like is not a good idea. Start where you are and look for the good in the present situation. I suffered from depression for years, and it was one of the best gifts I've ever been given. It led me to seek answers, which led me to a rich spiritual life, and I believe I am happier now than I would have been if I had never been depressed.

Look for the gift in your situation. I admit I can be hard, especially if you've been given something like a terminal diagnosis. I've known several people who went through this. Some of them went on to live long lives – and some didn't. The measure of success wasn't whether they died from their illness, but whether they received the blessings from the situation and were living from a peaceful, happy place during the time they were in their body. Granted, the ones I know who lived definitely did shift their vibration, but some of those who shifted their vibration still died early. We need to be open to mystery. Some reasons are beyond what we can understand on this plane of existence. Abraham says that if we die, we chose to – just maybe not consciously.

MISCONCEPTION

If I don't get what I wanted, I have failed.

Be open to different ways that your desires can be met. The truth is, becoming a happier person is all we really want. When you get so stuck on the form that the happiness comes in, it's hard to achieve. I've seen some people shift their vibration and add lots of joy to their lives, only to lose it because they became upset when their desires didn't manifest within a certain time frame. If you are happier, then you have succeeded and you are likely to manifest all that you desire – and more – over time, if you maintain that higher vibration.

Smarmy Ways The Law Of Attraction Has Been Twisted For Profit

Would you believe an ad in the back of a magazine that said this?

Miracle Pill!

Take one pill a day! Eat anything you want and lose thirty pounds a month! No exercise or lifestyle change necessary! Only $99.95! Order Today!

Then why would anyone believe an ad that said this?

Magic Affirmations!

Say these affirmations ten times a day and you'll get everything you want within one month! You don't have to do anything else! Say the affirmations and wait for your dreams to come true! Only $99.95! Order Today!

These types of ads cater to desperation. When you are desperate to make money, lose weight, find love or get the law of attraction to work, you are not going to attract the solution. That doesn't mean all law of attraction programs are crap – some of them are absolutely wonderful – but you probably won't find them when you are in a low or negative vibration state. I hate seeing so many obviously gross misinterpretations of the law of attraction designed simply to prey on people in order to make a quick buck.

Don't get me wrong, I think people who teach the law of attraction should make money for their efforts. I believe good teachers and coaches are worth every penny, but you have to be savvy. I even believe that some ancient mantras have a high vibration state attached to them, if for no other reason than the belief and faith of so many people over the years. These mantras seem to work like magic, and you can find them for free on the internet. Do a little research, read some free articles and get yourself in a vibration to attract something good before you pull your wallet out.

Where The Letter Writer Went Wrong

Let's reflect back on the letter. When I receive a letter like the one at the beginning of this chapter, I'm not surprised that the law of attraction isn't working for the author – their focus is all out of whack.

There are three classic law of attraction flubs that I see in this example. The first is that the letter writer thinks if everyone else changes, her life will be better – when really, she is the one who needs to change. Secondly, she is focused entirely on actions and not feelings. Actions are only helpful when they help us shift our feelings and vibration. Finally, she seems to be focusing only on what's wrong – not what's right about her life. I can't blame her, because many law of attraction teachings just skim the surface. To really change our lives, we need to go deeper.

My Magical Life Or Why the Law of Attraction Is Not Enough To Create The Life Of Your Dreams

My life isn't perfect, but I'm happy way more often than not. Sometimes, I'm downright blissful. I have a healthy body and I love how I look in the mirror. I have a loving husband and four kids that are pretty terrific. I was able to quit my teaching job when I was pregnant with our first child and help my husband run a heating and air conditioning business that we started from scratch in our garage. I've been able to spend lots of time holding and loving my babies, and I'm lucky enough to be able to homeschool them now.

We live in a really nice house with a gorgeous pool and palm trees in our backyard. I work about fifteen hours a week, and while my husband works a lot during our busy season, in the spring and fall he's often home by noon. We travel, we relax and enjoy life. I still have lots of experiences I want to create and areas where I can grow, but I consider my life successful, and I look forward to enjoying it more and more.

If we rewind back twenty-one years, my life looked very different. I was deeply depressed. I was teaching in a school with a principal I was sure was out to make life miserable and had an assistant who gave new meaning to the words "passive aggressive." The school system had sent me kids from a private, special-needs school without giving me the tools I needed to teach them in a public school setting that didn't welcome them.

I had postponed graduate school because I was sure my boyfriend of three years would propose if we both had jobs and a steady income. Instead, he cheated on me with his high school girlfriend when he went home for the holidays. Shortly after I found out and we decided to try to work through it, I came home to find him lying in the bathtub, spurting blood where he had slit his wrists and stabbed himself in the stomach in a suicide attempt. His parents came and took him away to a mental health facility in their hometown... and I was alone.

Alone in a job I hated, in a town I hated, where I knew only a few people. My family was eight hours away, in a town where it was very unlikely for me to find a teaching job. I couldn't go home. There was no one for me to lean on. My credit card bills were growing because I couldn't afford to pay the bills without my boyfriend's help. I was so low at this point in my life that I surrendered. I accepted the pain I was feeling and I let life suck. As I gained strength, I decided I was going to change my life, and I found the solutions.

Over time, I created a more and more joyful life. I did this long before I learned about the law of attraction. My transformation began twenty-one years ago, and I only learned about the law of attraction six years prior to writing these words. When I did learn about it, I was already doing many of the practices taught as law of attraction techniques, but I also had other elements in play that I believe made the law of attraction techniques work for me.

Now that I've shared with you why the law of attraction isn't enough to create the life of your dreams, don't despair – because I'm going to share with you the missing ingredient that will improve your success in your law of attraction practices.

BONUS!

Sign up and receive your free audio:

- What is the Difference Between Alchemy and Law of Attraction

dailyalchemy.com/personal-alchemy-book/

Main Points

- There are lots of misconceptions about the law of attraction.

- The law of attraction is just one of many laws at work in our universe.

- The law of attraction means you attract experiences, people and items into your life that match what you are vibrating.

- The best way to work with the law of attraction is to focus on changing your vibration.

- Law of attraction techniques alone are not enough to create the life of your dreams.

Chapter Two:

The Law of Attraction is Not Enough to Create the Life of Your Dreams

From the last chapter, you know that the law of attraction brings you experiences that match the feeling state you're generating, that match who you are at that moment. There are some law of attraction techniques that are designed to shift your feelings and/or vibrations – these usually work best to attract positive experiences. However, even more is required to create a change in your vibration which is significant enough to change your life.

How the Law of Attraction Works When You are Just Trying to Attract

If you are attracting what you want, then it seems the law of attraction is working perfectly, right? If you are trying to find a good parking spot or the perfect sweater, I would agree. All you need to do is attract it and it's yours. However, most of our bigger dreams require more than just attraction. It may be just as easy to manifest a castle as it is to manifest a button, as Abraham-Hicks says, but it takes a little more to hold onto the castle.

For example, look at these stories from a "true law of attraction stories" website:

On a dating site, I found a beautiful brunette. In her picture she was standing indoors (probably at home), smiling. She was slim, with long black curly hair. So I saved the picture and printed it out. Around this time, I bought vision board software and found a quote from the software to use with the picture: "I deserve the perfect partner, who I am now attracting."

During this period, nothing was happening in my life. I had just gotten out of a relationship, and I had no direction on where life was heading. So I decided to focus and put time and effort into my search for a partner. I both visualized on the picture and read the affirmation repeatedly. In some visualizations, I held her arms and kissed her. It felt very real. I did this often over the next two months. I truly believed she was my girlfriend.

A few months into this, I went to a nightclub with three friends. Two of them walked to the bar for drinks. While I was chatting with the other friend, a girl tapped my shoulder. I turned around and she looked just like the girl from the picture! Long, curly-haired brunette. She was slim, wore a long black elegant dress and tall heels. This girl was gorgeous!

She asked if I could take a picture of her and her friend. I agreed, and did just that. She thanked me, and then walked away. Minutes later, she came back and asked for a second picture. At this point, I knew she wanted me to make a move – I saw she was with several other people, any of whom could have taken the picture.

I was very shy back then. So things were difficult.

She thanked me after the second picture, and again walked away. Right after, I told my buddy, "This girl looks exactly like the one I've been visualizing." He was shocked.

Minutes later she returned for a third picture – I didn't speak up, took the picture, and she walked away again. After that, she disappeared, and I never saw her again.

Girls have approached me in the past, but never three times in a row like that. This girl tried three times – as if she truly believed I was her dream guy. I guess my visualizations were strong and the universe responded accordingly.

This made me a true believer in the law of attraction.

— www.positvethinking3.com

Here's another story from the same website:

On Craigslist, I created a personals ad. I also wanted to be a celebrity.

All I thought was "I'm a celebrity, and girls will be staring me down. I hope my appearance is camera ready!"

Sometimes women gave me attention. Whenever they did, I believed they recognized me from hit movies and TV shows. It helped with my belief of "being a celebrity."

Two weeks after creating the Craigslist ad and Hollywood celebrity story, I received an email from the television network Slice TV.

They wanted to interview me for a new reality dating show. I didn't respond, due to shyness. Some of my friends were upset with me for not going after this fun opportunity.

— www.positvethinking3.com

There's nothing wrong with either of these stories. They show the law of attraction working – these people attracted what they wanted to create in their lives. Still, the writers of these stories didn't get the girl or become a celebrity. They were missing the magic ingredient that makes the law of attraction work to create lasting change in our lives. Before I tell you what that ingredient is, I want to share another story with you about someone who has this ingredient, but doesn't try consciously to employ law of attraction techniques:

Fred is a young guy in his early twenties. He has always been upbeat, fun and likeable. He believes in following his heart and treating other people right. He's always wanted to be a chef and decided to follow that passion, even though his parents warned him he probably couldn't expect to earn much money. He attended one of the best culinary schools and studied pastry making in Europe. He was then able to get a job at a little bakery as the head chef – OK, as the only chef (it was, after all, only a little bakery). He auditioned for – and won – a cooking competition show on the Food Network. He met an investor who loved his pastries. The investor took him on limo rides and out on his yacht. The investor decided that he wanted to be Fred's silent partner, and helped him open a bakery. Fred had wanted to open a business of his own and suddenly got the opportunity to be a partner in his own bakery because of his expertise. His silent partner was putting up all the money, which had been the only thing standing between him and his dream.

Over the course of the next year, they opened three locations, plus a food truck and a kiosk at a local mall. Fred subsequently appeared on two more Food Network shows. He often volunteers for charities, teaching kids how to cook and garden. He's often featured in local and state news. His food has been served at many prominent events. He tells his mom, "Everybody loves me. I'm just a nice guy who makes cupcakes, what's not to love?"

The people in the first example are actively working law of attraction techniques, and while they are attracting, they're not really creating the life of their dreams. They haven't made themselves into the people they need to be to actually receive the experiences they want to attract. This shows that if you don't believe you are worthy of what you want to attract, you might attract it – but it won't stay in your life.

Fred didn't even know about the law of attraction, but he believed in following his passions and treating other people as well as he could, all while his dreams were coming true, as if by magic.

What's the difference? What's the magic ingredient that makes law of attraction techniques actually work, *and* helps create the life of your dreams – even if you've never heard of the law of attraction? *Personal Alchemy.*

What Is Alchemy?

Alchemy is a term that, like the law of attraction, has many different definitions and its exact meaning can be a little tricky to nail down. Many people think of an old medieval sage with a long beard, slaving over beakers full of mysterious substances, trying to turn lead into gold. There's much more to it than that. If I were writing this book in the 1500s, when alchemy was popular, I would probably be ranting about the term "alchemy" instead of taking issue with how the phrase "law of attraction" is often misunderstood. At that time, so many people were using "alchemy" to trick people for personal gain, or trying to (selfishly) create gold or immortality, it frustrated true alchemists, those who sought to understand the nature of the practice for its own sake. Even then, many people didn't understand the true purpose of alchemy. Alchemy can have as many definitions as the law of attraction.

Google defines alchemy as:

> *The medieval forerunner of chemistry, based on the supposed transformation of matter. It was concerned particularly with attempts to convert base metals into gold, or to find a universal elixir.*

While it's true that alchemy was a forerunner to chemistry, it was not primarily concerned with converting lead into gold. Alchemists were more concerned with transforming the leaden parts of themselves into metaphorical gold, changing themselves into better, more spiritual people. Many analogies were used in their writings, often using coded language to keep lay people from deciphering their hard won discoveries. This was because alchemists knew that if a person of a lower vibration, someone without the appropriate mindset, worked with some of these concepts, they would not get good results.

One of the big differences between alchemy and chemistry was the intent of the practitioner. In alchemy, the practitioner plays a big role in the outcome of any experiment. In chemistry, it is believed that any person can get the same result if they follow the same experimental procedure, but alchemists believed the outcome was influenced by the vibration of the person. They guarded their experiments and didn't let others see or touch them, lest the vibrations be changed. Here's a great, easy-to-understand definition from spiritsjourney.net:

> *[Alchemy is] any magical power or process of transmuting a common substance, usually of little*

value, into a substance of great value, a medieval chemical science and speculative philosophy aiming to achieve the transmutation of base metals into gold, the discovery of a universal cure for disease, and the discovery of a means of indefinitely prolonging life.

Ancient Alchemical Symbols and their oft times cryptic meanings began out of necessity as alchemists disguised their practices from the hugely powerful European church. At the height of its practice, alchemy was considered a heretical craft by the church, punishable by death (or worse, torture). The church body at the time viewed alchemy as a way for the practitioner to ascend to salvation outside of "traditional" church methodology.

Although ancient alchemical symbols were born out of this necessity, the foundation of alchemical practice is based on inner transformation, and the achievement of that transformation. As a means for this transmutation, the alchemist utilized the changing properties of matter in addition to the philosophical meanings of the symbols themselves.

The very act of turning base metals to gold is a symbol of (wo)man's ascension and achievement of enlightenment. All things, no matter how banal, hold deeper spiritual symbolic meaning to the alchemist in all of us.

As this definition explains, alchemy has to do with transformation. In fact, my favorite short definition of alchemy is found in Dennis William Hauck's, *Complete Idiot's Guide to Alchemy*:

The art of transformation.

Alchemists believed that spiritual growth and transformation naturally occur over time as we evolve, but they wanted to speed up the process and transform faster.

Where Did the Law of Attraction Come From and What Does it Have to Do with Alchemy?

The law of attraction may be a term that came into vogue only in recent years, but it's been around forever. Surprisingly enough the first recorded reference to the law of attraction, "as above, so below; as within, so without," comes from the first recorded alchemical writing, *The Emerald Tablet*. This tablet is even briefly mentioned in the law of attraction movie, *The Secret*. The tablet is allegedly similar to the tablets the Ten Commandments were supposedly written on. Both have been lost, but we still have the words that were written on them, and both hold great meaning to the people who study them.

The Emerald Tablet was said to have been composed in ancient Egypt. The oldest know translation was written in Arabic, sometime between the sixth and eighth century. It has continued to show up in literature throughout time, even though the actual tablet has been lost. C.G. Jung claimed to have dreams and visions about the tablet, and many famous alchemists created their own translations, including Isaac Newton.

All alchemists worth their salt have studied *The Emerald Tablet*. It's the basis for all alchemical teachings, and also the basis for law of attraction techniques. For many years, the two were taught as part of a whole, but now people are being taught only part of these truths. The law of attraction is not complete without alchemy – not if you want to significantly change your life. Some people who have never heard of alchemy are able to manifest through studying only the law of attraction, but I believe those people are unwittingly changing their personal alchemy as they work within the confines of law of attraction.

While, as a spiritual alchemist, I find the history and tradition of alchemy fascinating, most people don't need extensive study in the subject. Just by knowing that the law of attraction is part of alchemy, and by working with the two together, you can completely transform your life.

What Is Personal Alchemy?

If you start researching alchemy, you will find that there are many different types – spiritual alchemy, physical alchemy, plant alchemy (or spagyrics)... the list goes on. There are just as many types of transformations that can be made through alchemy.

Personal alchemy, as you may have guessed, is the art or science of transforming yourself. It's the most important kind of alchemy, and technically, it is the aim of all alchemy. The alchemist who works with creating plant tinctures does so not only to transform the plant into medicine, but to transform himself as he transforms the plant. "As above, so below."

We can do the same thing by just working on our own personal alchemy. It used to take years of work to make subtle changes for most alchemists, but time moves faster now. We don't have to spend years meditating to shift our vibration. Often, we can begin to make shifts in one session. All the work done by previous generations has made the path easier for the rest of us.

Personal Alchemy is not so much transforming yourself as allowing your true self to emerge. It focuses on getting your own vibration as close to the vibration of your higher self as possible. As this happens, everything changes. Many alchemists of the past died because they worked with mercury, lead, and other poisonous substances. The alchemist who had spent many years raising his vibration was affected differently and had different results from these experiments. The toxic chemicals did not harm him, because his vibration was so high. Luckily, there is no need for any of us to deal with toxic chemicals. Just by shifting our vibration we can get totally different results from our law of attraction techniques. We may even find that we don't need those techniques as much, or at all.

How Can Personal Alchemy Change Your Life?

Personal alchemy will change your life whether or not you consciously engage in law of attraction techniques. Personal alchemy can be practiced in conjunction with other religious beliefs, and it can be practiced by those who have no spiritual beliefs at all. If you use personal alchemy only and not the law of attraction, you can be like Frank earlier in the chapter, who created a magic life without doing anything other than being himself and following his bliss.

If you do want to incorporate both personal alchemy and the law of attraction into your life, you will see magic occur. For example, let's say you find a magic wand. Sometimes it works, sometimes it doesn't—and you don't really know why. Then, a great wizard holds the wand and it does everything he says. This wand is like the law of attraction and the wizard is personal alchemy. The power of the wand is affected by the user, just like the power of the law of attraction is affected by the personal alchemy of the practitioner. The magic wand may have power by itself, but (like any tool) when wielded by someone who has great personal power and skill, the results will be magnified.

You are an Ingredient in Every Recipe You Cook

I'd like to share one more analogy about how personal alchemy works. This one relates to cooking. Kitchen alchemy is actually a potent form of alchemy and everyone who cooks uses it to some degree whether they are aware of it or not. It's one of my favorite things to play with.

Have you noticed that food tastes differently depending on who cooked it? Does your mom say that her magic ingredient is love? Surely you've noticed that two different people who follow the same recipe will not have the exact same results. They will probably be similar, unless the recipe is very complex, but never exactly the same. Part of this is because of differences in the chef's ability and style, the raw ingredients and cooking tools, such as the oven, etc. I would also contend that the results are affected by the vibration of the cook, how they feel about cooking, how they feel about who they are cooking for, and their intention for the outcome of the recipe. In other words, the cook is one of the ingredients in the recipe and plays a big part in the result. Personal alchemy touches every part of our lives, because we put ourselves into everything we do.

Although there is much more to alchemy that can be covered in this short e-book, it doesn't matter because just like the law of attraction, alchemy is at work in your life whether you know it or not. Most of what you will read in the next few chapters is not traditional alchemy. I'm not going to ask you to read a bunch of esoteric, ancient writings or grind herbs. Instead, I'm going to give you some simple ways that you can focus on connecting with your higher self and raising your vibration so your life flows better with or without the law of attraction techniques.

Main Points

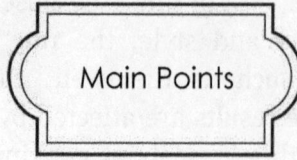

- The Law of Attraction works but it's not enough to give you the life of your dreams.

- If you attract something you don't feel worthy of having, you won't be able to keep it.

- *The Emerald Tablet*, an ancient alchemical text, is the first known writing about the law of attraction and alchemy.

- The Law of Attraction brings you what you are vibrating; alchemy changes how you vibrate.

- Your personal alchemy can change how the law of attraction works for you.

- You are an ingredient in every recipe you cook.

Chapter Three:

Personal Alchemy Starts with You

Have you ever read a how-to book and still had no clue how the person in the book achieved what they did, or what to do yourself? I've experienced this often as an aspiring writer and blogger. For example, I read an e-book on how to get 50,000 blog followers, and while I followed the suggestions and employed all of the writer's recommended techniques, I didn't have the same results. Why not? Because I wasn't her, I wasn't vibrating the same way she was. Often, we might think that writers of how-to books are holding back and not telling us the elusive secret that made them successful. They aren't – because many of them don't realize it themselves. It's the secret I shared with you in the last chapter: you are an ingredient in every recipe you bake.

I can follow the exact same steps as she did, but I won't necessarily get similar results unless I'm vibrating in a similar way. Her techniques may have been great, and quite a few of them were definitely things I needed to do to grow my blog's readership, but I also needed to be aware that until I was vibrating at a similar frequency, I wouldn't get the same kind of results.

It doesn't mean that I won't get results, or that it's not worth my time to take the recommended actions, but it does mean that I might want to focus more on my personal alchemy.

Abraham-Hicks says "the moment you desire something, it appears in your vortex" and that's true. All of your desires are already there, just waiting for you to line up with them. One of the fastest and most fulfilling ways to do that is through personal alchemy. The great bonus is that when you work on transforming yourself, you often experience so much joy that you don't worry about manifesting, and ironically enough that's often when things begin to happen.

I've experienced my share of disappointments in my writing career, even though I put pictures of my stories selling on my vision board, wrote the story of my success in present tense every day, and pretended I was already a famous author. Still, the rejections rolled in. At one point, I decided to totally stop focusing on my writing and cease practicing any law of attraction techniques for a solid week. During that week, I focused on self-love, relaxing and enjoying my life. A few days later, I was feeling a lot of bliss, and not really trying to create anything. While I was in this state, Pam Grout, author of *E-Squared*, offered to interview me on her blog. During that process, I found that I had a magical experience doing one of the experiments from Pam's book.

I was trying to see a white feather and I ended up seeing over a hundred thousand white feathers. When I told this story to Jeannette Maw, the creator of Good Vibe University, she had me write a guest post about it for her Good Vibe Blog. Pam then asked me to go on a radio show with her to tell my story. I had the most web traffic I'd ever seen to my blog that week from all the mentions and guest posts. When I stopped trying to visualize my writing career moving forward, and focused instead on loving myself, I had a magical week. Those experiences were beyond what I could have thought to ask for, but they were perfect, and made me excited to write again.

How to Begin to Transform Yourself

Personal alchemy starts with you and how you are vibrating. Traditional alchemical transformation follows seven steps which are designed to get to the pure essence of the object. Alchemists are attempting to purify either the herb, the metal, or themselves. They go through steps to get rid of what does not belong, by burning and distilling, and they continue taking away any excess until what is left is the pure vibration of the object.

Even though we are talking about transformation, we are, like the other alchemists, attempting to purify our vibration and get to our true selves. We are not really trying to change ourselves into something we are not, but to focus on the highest, golden part of ourselves, so that we can begin to vibrate from that part of us and let go of the old leaden vibrations we no longer need. This may sound very esoteric, but everything has a vibration. In his book *Power vs. Force,* David R. Hawkins explains the different vibrational levels of things, such as rock music & classical music, and how they affect us. People are able to raise their vibrations by choosing their thoughts, actions and what and who they interact with.

There are three aspects of personal alchemy that we are going to focus on in this book. In this chapter, we will look at ways to raise our own vibrations through our interactions with ourselves. In the next chapters, we will focus on our interactions with others and our universe.

I will share seven exercises that loosely correspond to the seven steps of traditional alchemy for each of these three areas. You don't have to follow all of them or do them in order to reap the benefits. Follow your feelings, do the ones that feel good to you. Just remember, if you've been trained to not love yourself, doing these activities will feel strange at first. Keep at it and in time they will be your ticket to bliss.

Worthiness

Exercise 1: Your Statement Of Being

I first learned about personal mission statements twenty years ago from Steven Covey's book, *The Seven Habits of Highly Effective People*. Personal mission statements are a great guide to keep you on track to follow the big picture goals in your life. However, in personal alchemy, we want to go even deeper and create a statement of being. It not only has to do with your mission in life, but who you choose to be while you're on this planet. You may think that you don't get to decide this. You may believe that fate or God chose that for you or that if you existed in the non-physical and chose to be who you are today, that there's nothing you can do about it now.

In reality, you were given some clay. The clay might be soft or hard, dark or light, but it's just the raw material you get to use to create yourself. You may have a disease or a disability. We all have some limitations that we work within due to the clay we were given, but that doesn't limit the creative ways in which we can be who we want to be. It's pretty simple actually – you make a decision about who you want to be and then you start being that person.

I love how Gabourey Sidibe, an actress, describes a decision she made about herself:

> *One day, I decided that I was beautiful, and so I carried out my life as if I was a beautiful girl. I wear colors that I really like, I wear makeup that makes me feel pretty, and it really helps. It doesn't have anything to do with how the world perceives you. What matters is what you see. Your body is your temple, it's your home, and you must decorate it.*

She didn't look for someone else to make the decision for her or tell her she was beautiful. She decided it for herself, and that's how she began to move through the work. That is the kind of decision that can totally shift your personal alchemy.

Also, we must remember that along with our limitations, we all have gifts. If you don't think you have special talents and abilities, you're wrong. There are so many things that only you can do in this world. Remember: you are an ingredient in every cake you bake. No one can do it just like you. Don't hold back when you create your statement of being.

My original personal mission statement was this:

To teach unconditional love through thoughts, words, and actions.

My current statement of being:

I am a radiant, beautiful, magical author, alchemist and teacher who expands the joy, love, magic and delight in my life and the lives of those I touch.

Which one seems more inspiring? To me, when I read my statement of being it ignites my excitement to go out into the world and be me.

Here are a few simple steps to creating your own statement of being:

1) *Start with the words "I am,"* then list who you have decided to be in the world. Then, add the word "who" and fill in what you are going to do in the world.

2) *Think big.* You are already impacting the world every single day. You might as well decide how you want to do it.

3) Once you get it written in a way that makes you smile, *memorize it* as well as write it down in places you will later see it.

4) Follow your decisions and be who you have decided to be. No one can stop you.

Don't share it with anyone unless you are 100% sure they will be supportive.

Exercise 2: Daily Love List

Love is a verb, and you need to show yourself loving actions daily. This sends a message to your subconscious and your body that you love yourself. When you give yourself love your body is healthier, your mind is more compliant, and you sabotage yourself less often. I have a daily love list for myself and this is one of the exercises that I do every day. I either do the activities on my list or some other, better options.

Lisa Hayes, the Love Whisperer, calls this her "Sacred Ten," and says that we need a list of at least ten activities that we will do for ourselves each day. I think you can find the amount that works for you – it might be three, five, ten or even fifteen. Sometimes, such as when you're on vacation, you may have time to do more.

I have a little laminated checklist for mine that I keep on a clipboard and actually check off each item as I complete it with a dry erase marker. You might want to put yours on your computer or on a sticky note on your bathroom mirror – anywhere you'll see it and remember to do it each day. It might feel better to have a pre-made list, or just to keep a tally every day of what you did from your love list that day. Try to do at least one or two things within a few minutes of waking.

Here's a list of some ideas to get you started with creating your own list:

Meditate	Savor a cup of coffee/tea
Apply lotion to yourself, sending your body love	Play a video game or a cool app on your phone
Sniff an essential oil	Burn a candle you like
Eat a piece of good chocolate	Listen and/or dance to your favorite music
Take your vitamins	Talk to a friend
Go for a walk	Take a hot bubble bath
Take a shower by candlelight	Wear something you feel good in
Paint	Draw
Write	Journal
Watch an episode of your favorite TV show	Watch a TED talk on YouTube
Eat something you love	Take a nap
Listen to an audio book	Go to the gym
Read a chapter of a juicy novel	Do yoga
Ride your bike	Play tennis

The only rule is that they have to be things that make you feel good when you do them. If going to the gym is drudgery to you, then that's not an activity for this list. One of the things on my list is dry brushing my skin every morning before I get in the shower. It's good for my lymphatic system, it makes my skin feel good, and wakes me up in the morning.

Everyone's list will be individual and will shift and change over time. Occasionally, you might find that you need to change your list, add or change the items on it to amp up the love feelings you get from it. If you go to have a massage one day, then you might not need to do any of the other things on your list that day because that was a big item. Use your own judgment, but show yourself tangible acts of love every day. Once you have your list complete, make sure you do as many of the items a day as you can, and do it mindfully with the intention of giving yourself love. Don't beat yourself up if you miss a day, or can't get to everything on the list – that defeats the point of the exercise, which is to be more loving to yourself. Just start fresh the next day.

Exercise 3: Eye Gazing

This exercise may feel silly, but it's very powerful and it can shift how you feel about yourself. Find a quiet time when you can be alone with a mirror. Then I want you to take three minutes to stare into your own eyes with the intention of sending yourself love. You can do it by thinking of how you feel when you look into your lover's eyes, your child's eyes or even imagine God looking into your eyes.

If it's hard to do, set a timer. You may find lots of emotions coming up – and that's fine. If you haven't done this before, it can be tricky. I want you to try to do this as a meditation. Try not to think about anything but sending love to the eyes you are looking into. If you can't see well enough to do this, you can do it in your mind, trying to imagine what your eyes look like, and visualize yourself looking into them.

Do this exercise every day for at least two weeks. If you like it, you might want to add it to your daily love list.

Exercise 4: Feel Your Feelings

We often beat ourselves up over any feeling that we deem negative, especially if we practice law of attraction techniques, but we have feelings for a reason. Feelings are a gift. They let us know how we are thinking and vibrating, and they help us process difficult experiences. Let yourself feel your feelings and accept them, no matter what they are.

I usually do an abbreviated version of the Sedona Method by Hale Dwoskin to feel my feelings. I ask myself if I can be fully present with this feeling. Then, once I feel I've felt it as deeply as I can, I ask myself if I can let it go. Whatever the answer, yes or no, I usually find myself letting it go, at least a little. The funny thing is, once I learned to do this with joyful feelings, it seemed that after I felt the feeling fully and let it go, it would get even more intense. From my experience, any feeling fully felt takes you to a higher place on the vibrational scale.

Set a time at least once a day for five minutes to really feel your feelings. If you have a lot of scary feelings that you've been hiding from, you might think they will never go away if you start mindfully, intentionally feeling them – but the opposite is true. The rule is that you have to feel your feelings, not think about why they are there. Don't let a narrative run in your head about why you are angry or mad or sad. Just feel the feeling in your body and ask yourself the two questions.

Exercise 5: Love Talk

Whole books have been written about this technique – it's that important. You are talking to yourself inside your head all day long – we all narrate our lives for ourselves to a large extent, and that narration tells us what kind of story we're in. It's beyond important how you talk to yourself. How do you think Gandhi talked to himself? Do you think he put himself down? Think of any powerful person who has made big changes in the world, and talk to yourself as you believe they would talk to themselves. We can't put ourselves down, and be who we want to be in the world at the same time. Talk to yourself the way you would to someone you love and admire. Hopefully, if you don't yet love and admire yourself, you soon will.

Take some time every day to give yourself a pep talk. Then as you go through your day, remember to keep talking positively to yourself. If you slip up and catch yourself being critical, just start over. Some of us have been trained to talk down to ourselves since we were toddlers. We don't have to change it overnight. Let it slowly become a new habit.

Here's a sample script to give you an idea:

> *Today is going to be a great day. You are doing such a great job shifting the way you talk and think about yourself. I'm so proud of you. We are feeling fabulous today and we're going to drive this car through town like the fabulous creator that we are. I love the way you organized our day, and I love that you were brave and sent that resume out. New and wonderful things are coming our way, and I'm so excited. Thanks for the wonderful way you take care of us.*

It may feel a little odd, but it will do you way more good than going through your day saying things like "I can't believe you screwed that up," or "Things are never going to change for me."

Exercise 6: Love Your Cells

You are made up of at least 50% water (some studies say up to 80%!) and composed of lots of tiny vibrating atoms that make up the cells in your body. Vibrating atoms make up the entirety of your body. This fact, combined with the knowledge I learned from Dr. Masaru Emoto's water study, led me to create this exercise. Dr. Emoto took samples of water and placed them into containers. On some containers he wrote uplifting words like "love," "gratitude," "peace," and "truth." On other containers he wrote negative phrases like "you fool," "you disgust me" and "evil." He then froze the samples and took pictures of the water crystals that formed. The water that was exposed to positive phrases formed beautiful snowflake shapes, but the ones exposed to negative words looked like ugly blobs. He also did this experiment with different types of music, pictures and prayers with a similar outcome. If we are mainly made up of water, then wouldn't we be as affected by the words around us?

I decided to try two things. One is that I meditate and visualize the cells in my body, and the water in them. During my meditation I speak words of love to my cells and I visualize myself writing words on my cells. Sometimes I might choose "love," other times it might be "peace" or "prosperity" depending on what I would like to vibrate more of at that moment. I then visualize that word copying itself and spreading to all the billions of cells in my body.

I have experienced feelings of total bliss after doing this type of meditation. Give it a try, and you'll find that sending love to the cells in your body can shift your mood quickly.

As an additional bonus activity, try wearing a t-shirt with a positive word or phrase such as "love" and see if you feel a shift when you intend to connect with the water in your body. If you can't find a t-shirt with the phrase you want, you can even write it with marker somewhere on your body. If you are really attached to one, you could even get a tattoo. Knowing about Dr. Emoto's study makes me wonder about the impact some people's tattoos have on their vibration, both good and bad.

Exercise 7: Vibration Mixology

While we each have an overall vibration set point, we also vibrate differently on different subjects. Some of us might easily allow love into our lives, but can't seem to make money. I personally have an easy time in the love and money departments, but I've had to focus a little more when I went to have success with my creative endeavors.

Once you've been doing some of these exercises and you find your overall vibration is rising higher, you may want to focus on raising your vibration on certain specific subjects. Luckily, we all usually have some area of life that comes easy for us.

For this exercise, I want you to first think of something that comes easy for you and that you feel good about. It could be something general like your career or more specific like your car which always runs perfectly. Focus on that thought, and feel the vibration of how wonderful that part of your life is in your open right hand. Then in your open left hand, experience the vibration of how you feel in the area of your life that you want to improve. Go back and forth between feeling the two vibrations a few times in your mind. Then place your right hand on top of your left, and mix the higher vibration into the lower.

The result will be a mix that is somewhere between the two vibrations. Next, intend for that vibration to be the new vibration for the area you were focusing on improving. I've found improvement in more difficult areas of life were shifted to better, higher vibration states simply through this exercise, without doing anything else.

If it's hard for you to feel the vibration, just pretend. You can also get my free "shift your vibration" kit on my blog, at www.dailyalchemy.com. The kit has been designed with the intention of guiding you through learning to feel your vibrations, and it's my gift to you.

Personal Alchemy Success Story

When I think of an example of success through personal alchemy, Taylor Hicks often come to mind. Taylor was the Season Five *American Idol* winner. He walked into the auditions and Simon, one of the judges, voted against him because he said that Taylor did not have "the look" – Taylor had a head full of prematurely gray hair – or the talent that would get him through the Hollywood Round. He had a good voice, but it wasn't extraordinary. Still, the other two judges voted for him, and he made it to the next round.

Not only did he make it to the top ten, he had his own group of very loyal fans called "The Soul Patrol." Many people were amazed when he won because he didn't represent the traditional "pop star persona" that normally wins. He stayed true to just being who he was and it resonated with the voters. Most people with similar talents wouldn't have made it through the first round, but he made it all the way to the top, and now has a great career because of it. Why? Because of who he is and how he vibrates – his level of personal alchemy.

Let it Be Easy

Learning to love yourself and shifting your thoughts about who you are doesn't have to be difficult. Just take it one step at a time, and don't criticize yourself for not being perfect. The way to transform yourself is to be okay with who you are right now, and allow more of your higher self that already exists to express itself through you.

The goal of these exercises is that you will begin to adore yourself, that your heart will skip a beat when you see yourself in the mirror, the way it did when you saw your beloved after falling in love for the first time. That your heart will melt for yourself like it did for your newborn baby the first time you held it in your arms.

You are precious, and it's important that you feel it to your core, not just for yourself but for all of us in this universe.

BONUS!

Sign up and receive your free audios and PDFs.

- Vibe-Mixology Intro Audio
- Daily Love List Planning Form & Audio

dailyalchemy.com/personal-alchemy-book/

Main Points

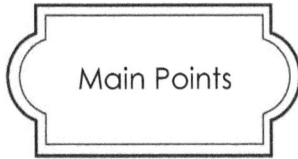

- Your personal alchemy is how you are vibrating in the world.

- You can improve your personal alchemy through three areas of focus: yourself, other people and the universe.

- Personal Alchemy work helps you to let go of the vibrations that no longer serve you and express more of your true self.

- A Statement of Being reminds you of who you have decided to be and what you have decided to do in the world.

- Daily acts of love for yourself are important.

- Allow yourself to feel your feelings.

- Develop a habit of talking positively to yourself.

- Our cells need love and positive thoughts, too.

- We vibrate differently on different subjects.

- Let change be easy. Don't work hard at it. Keep it light and fun.

Chapter Four:

We're Not In It By Ourselves

In the last chapter, we focused on our own vibration, and that is definitely key to personal transformation.

However, we aren't here alone on the planet, and often our interaction with each other brings the biggest challenges to our growth. After you spend some time focusing on strengthening your self-love muscles, it will be time to add other people back into the mix. The best place to start is by increasing the love you feel towards others, just like you did for yourself.

Often, it's easier to focus on people in general than it is to focus on specific people in your life. There are less hurts to heal when you focus more generally – but you'll want to eventually focus on the people you know well, the people in your life, as there are big rewards for improving your feelings about them. You're going to do some experiments with both.

A lot of your success in life depends on other people's reactions to you and your work. Much of that reaction is based on your personal alchemy level. Zig Ziglar says, "You can have everything you want in life if you just help enough people get what they want." I would agree, but I think that your beliefs around why you are helping other people matter as well. You don't want to give just to receive because that takes away the joy you get from the act of giving. But you also don't want to give saying you expect nothing, because then that's probably what you'll get. Focus on increasing your joy and the joy of others. When you do this, your own vibration will transform, and you will be aiding in the transformation of others.

Other Ingredients In Your Recipes

You are always an ingredient in every recipe you cook, but you aren't the only ingredient. The vibration of your world, the other people involved in the project, and your desired outcome all affect your outcome, too.

I had an experience once when I had injured my ankle and wanted it to heal. I'm usually a very quick healer. It seems physical health is an area of high vibration for me, but in this case the ankle didn't want to heal. I was sending love to my cells and visualizing it healed, I was taking care of myself and relaxing, I was watching funny movies and playing board games with my kids. But in the back of my mind, I was thinking about how I needed this ankle to heal. I had places to go and things to do – my kids had to get to school, I had to go to work and get groceries, and do all the things I do in our household.

Finally, I decided to follow my own advice and relax and let the universe help me. My ankle was not hurt that badly and it would heal soon enough. For some reason, the idea came to mind that I should spend some time sending reiki (a type of healing energy) and love to other people who had ankle injuries, some way worse than mine. I knew what it felt like, so I had the utmost empathy. I sat for about an hour or so and sent reiki, with no thoughts of healing myself, to anyone who had an ankle injury.

Now, I didn't personally know anyone who currently had an ankle injury – I just intended for the reiki to reach the people who needed it. After doing this, I got up on my crutches and went to do some chores around the house. I slowly realized my ankle didn't hurt as much as I thought it did. In fact, by that evening I no longer needed crutches, and the swelling in my sprain was completely gone. By making a concerted effort to send healing energy to others, I had healed myself.

This can also happen in the opposite way. When you put such loving vibrations into something that you do, other people can feel it and they will be drawn to it. To me this explains why some books are runaway successes despite critics of the quality of the author's writing. Sometimes heart, passion and love trump talent. In fact, it often does, as illustrated by the story of Taylor Hicks in Chapter Two. He was not the most talented singer in the competition – but he won. This doesn't mean that talent isn't important or that you shouldn't do your best work or give your best performance, just don't feel that you have to be perfect to connect with other people. They feel the love and passion that you put into your work and that is what makes it popular – or not.

Highest Vibe Is In Control

In the book *Power vs. Force*, David Hawkins, states that one person vibrating at a level of, say, 800 or above will have more impact on the collective energy of our world than millions of people vibrating at 200 or below. By working on making your vibration rate or your feeling set point a higher level, you help all of humanity, and those who are at higher set points help you. Really let that soak in. By working on your own personal alchemy, you can help shift our whole planet and make life better for *everyone*. It's a pretty good reason to take on the challenge. It doesn't have to be hard – in fact, transforming through joy and love creates much more lasting and drastic transformation than changing by pushing hard.

The knowledge that residing at a higher set point, or even just vibrating higher at a certain moment in time, grants you power has made a significant change in how I interact with people. If you look at a map of consciousness that shows the power levels of different emotions (http://creativeculturelabs.com/power-vs-force-applications-to-creative-consciousness), you will notice that anger has more power than shame, fear, or guilt. This is the reason many fearful people find themselves at the mercy of angry people, and things finally begin to shift if the fearful people get angry, too. It gives them their power back.

The magic begins to happen when they go for higher levels of courage – neutrality or above. Once a person reaches these levels, they are above anger, and they can more easily navigate other people's anger, because they are coming from a place of greater power. I'm not talking about power as in the power to win an argument – when we reach that level, we don't have to fight. We will either not be bothered by the other person's anger, or the other person's anger will dissipate in the presence of a higher vibration. The more you focus on personal alchemy, the less conflict you have in your life.

I've heard stories of monks in India who spend years in caves mediating on love to help bring up the vibration of the planet and Carmelite nuns who do the same thing in their nunnery. Swami Balendu is a guru who spent three years in a cave meditating. Once he left the cave, he felt the equality of all and began traveling to share his loving energy with everyone he meets.

Exercise 1: See Them As God Does

In the previous chapter, I asked you to see yourself from God's perspective. Now, I'm asking you to see other people through God's eyes. We constantly judge others, but God does not. Imagine you are God looking at one of your creations with total compassion for all they have gone through and who they are. Talk to them, inside your head, as if you were God talking to them.

For example, "Look at you, my beautiful daughter. I love how you are expressing the energy that is you. You think you have a lot to learn, and people are mean, but I know you are going to be just fine, and that spark of love that created you cannot be covered up. I see it shining in your eyes. I love how you've pretended to forget who you are and play in this universe. I'm so glad I can observe the life that you live and how you put your whole self into the stories that you have created, and I know that you will keep creating stories that feel even better and better. I made a tricky illusion for you to work in, but you are doing great. Keep it up."

This will feel strange, and I would not share these thoughts out loud, but it will shift how you see other people and it can bring on a total bliss bomb. As for me, when I've done this in a discount store that is notorious for bad service and rude employees, I found myself crying because the cashiers were so beautiful and gave the best service imaginable.

Over time, one of the stores I used to dread shopping in transformed into a place where I know and love many of the employees. We know each other by name, I know about their kids and their families, and about what's important to them. It all started because once I looked on them with total love, then I couldn't help but smile and chat with them. Now I can't wait to hear how they are, and I always get wonderful service with a smile.

Here's a link to an audio that walks you through this exercise: https://soundcloud.com/michelle-martindobbins/seeing-through-gods-eyes

Exercise 2: Love List For Others

Just like we have a love list for ourselves, we should have one for other people. It doesn't have to be as detailed as our list for ourselves, but you want to have a concrete way to make sure that you're taking loving action for others in the world. I know we all do loving acts for our family and the people around us, but when we intend to increase the love vibration in our home, neighborhood, country or world, as we do it, it makes our results even more profound. Plan a way to do it that works for you. You could decide to do one act of kindness every day, or three acts a week. You might create a list of different actions like you did for your personal love list and see how many you can do each day or week.

Remembering the intent and the feeling as you do them is important. Don't do it to check it off your list, or pursue it in a way that makes it a burden. Do it to increase the amount of love you feel.

Here's a list of ideas to get you started:

Smile at strangers	Hold the door open for people
Put uplifting notes on cards and leave them where people will find them*	Put bubbles or sidewalk chalk in a park with a sign that says "Take me!"
Put warm coats and gloves out for homeless people to take in the winter	Put a treat in everyone's mail box or on their desk at work
Give somebody a loan through kiva.com	Donate to a homeless shelter or a soup kitchen
Pick someone a bouquet of flowers	Babysit for a friend who needs some time alone
Tutor a child who needs help in school	Visit a nursing home
Buy coffee or lunch for a stranger	Clean out your closets and donate items you no longer need
Read to a school class	Donate books to a library
Write positive reviews for authors you love	Look for people to uplift on social media
Help make someone's dream come true by donating at gofundme.com or kickstarter.com	

*Go to ripplekindness.com to look for ideas; print their kindness cards to give out

Exercise 3 Intercession (Positive Prayer)

Whether or not you believe in the power of prayer or are religious at all doesn't matter, you can still send positive energy to other people. Personally, I believe all of our thoughts are prayers, and the best way to pray for someone is to think good thoughts about them. When doing this, I picture the person I'm focusing on encased in a bubble of white light, surrounded by love, smiling and happy. If there is something I know they want, such as better health or a new job, I picture them experiencing what they want. If not, I just continue to picture them smiling and happy until the energy shifts, and then I go to the next person on my prayer list. I also pray for people in my neighborhood, town, state, etc. I picture these places filled with love and see joyful people.

The more we raise our vibration, the stronger our prayers become. Not because God listens to our pleas, but because our vibrations simply raise the set vibration of any place we focus on, once our vibration rises. I've read of studies where cities experienced lower crime rates when group meditations focused on it, or when holy people, like monks, moved into the city. We have more power for good than we realize.

Exercise 4: Sending Out the Love Vibes

This is similar to praying for people, but slightly different. It is something you do while you are doing other tasks that don't require your full attention. I like to do this while standing in line or driving my car. I simply take a few minutes to focus on loving thoughts until I find my vibration lifting, and then I picture sending that love out to anyone I see or any car that passes me on the road. When I do this on long car trips or in line at an amusement park where there are lots of people, I find myself feeling really energized and joyful.

I also like to think that maybe there have been less accidents on the road or incidents in places of business because of the boost in love energy. If I happen to see an ambulance, police car, accident or someone having an altercation, I send an extra boost of love their way. I often send reiki energy, and if you know any kind of energy healing technique you can send that – but if not, don't worry; nothing is more healing than pure love. This activity blesses everyone around you, and you can't help but feel all the love you are sending out, too.

Exercise 5: Talk to Their Higher Self

This sounds a lot more complicated than it is. You don't need to follow any specific rules but just sit down by yourself in a quiet place and intend to connect with the person's higher self and speak from your heart. I always make sure I can come from a loving place when I do this. Even if I am in disagreement with them, I have to be willing to hear their point of view and feel like I have everyone's best interest at heart.

I usually do this technique right before I go to bed, but you can do it in any quiet time. Sit down and meditate or quiet your thoughts as much as you can for a few minutes. Then, think about the person with whom you want to connect. Visualize them waving at you and smiling. If you are more of a feeling person, feel their energy. If you experience the world more intensely through sound, hear their voice.

I have had some miraculous results with this technique – I post about it on my Facebook page often, and I find more people ask me about it than almost any other technique I use. It really is a simple thing to do. I use the technique for one of two reasons: either I have lost touch with someone and I really want to reconnect but can't locate them or I've had a misunderstanding with someone and/or they are behaving in a way that hurts me, and I either have had no luck communicating directly with them, or there is a good reason not to.

If you are just trying to connect with someone you haven't seen for a long time, just ask your higher self and their higher self to find a way for one of you to find the other so you can reconnect. Then picture the two of you hugging and laughing after being reunited. After doing this, I had a college friend I hadn't seen in over ten years call me three days later.

If you are trying to connect with someone you are having a disagreement with, whether or not you are friends, picture yourself hugging the person or shaking hands if that would be more appropriate. Then ask your higher self to explain to their higher self that you mean them no harm, and would like to end the argument. Let them know you love them, and that you want to find a solution that lets everyone win. Be sure to only do this technique when you can feel at least neutral about the situation. If you do it from a place of anger or fear, your results may not be good. After doing this exercise, I have had friends I was in conflict with call me and act like nothing was amiss after not speaking to me for six months. A friend had a lawsuit dropped after doing this activity toward the person who was suing her. We are connected in ways that we can't always see and if we set the intention and are in the right vibration, we can connect through our higher selves.

Exercise 6: Love Their Flaws

It's easy to love the nice parts of people, but sometimes you have to do more than what is easy. In this exercise you will focus on two or more qualities that someone has, or actions that they have carried out that you dislike. Then, list three reasons while those qualities or actions could be good – even if you don't believe the reasons are valid or true in this case. Then, continue to do this every day until you feel a shift and can begin to feel love for the parts of the person that you dislike. Sometimes, it helps to see the qualities from the perspective of an outside observer that doesn't know you or the other person. Write the person a letter thanking them for those qualities or actions and telling them of the gifts you received because of them. If you don't see a gift, make one up but over time you will likely see the gift – since you have intended to do so. Once you are done with the letter, burn it or destroy it.

This obviously works well for people in our own lives, but it can also work well for celebrities or politicians we disagree with. It can shift our vibration greatly if we can get to a place of feeling love for a politician and a policy they created that we dislike. If we can learn to see the blessing in their actions, it can give us great freedom. For example, if a certain politician vetoed the clean water bill you were passionate about, perhaps you could see that maybe the funds needed to implement it weren't available, maybe there were parts of the bill that could be made stronger or better, maybe some of the components could be implemented by a private charity and keep down the amount of possible corruption. Maybe you would want to thank them because he or she gave you the opportunity to better study or understand the law and to learn more about the situation and how to improve it. In every perceived problem or flaw there is a gift. It's our job to find it.

Exercise 7: Vibration Mixology with Others

In this exercise, we are going to do a similar exercise from the last chapter where we mixed our own vibes on two different subjects to get the lower vibration to rise. In this case, we will mix our energy with the energy of someone else, even if just in our imagination.

If you know someone who is struggling and you want to send them a boost, you can do it by symbolically sharing your vibration with them. Sit and take time to center and feel your own vibration. (If you need help with this, you can get my free *Revamp Your Vibe* kit here: michellemartindobbins.com/get-your-happy-back/

Before starting, I always intend that my own vibration will stay where it is or go higher as a result of doing this exercise. Then, once you feel you are in a really good feeling space, you can try to sense the other person's vibration. Picture them holding out their hand and you placing your hand on top of theirs, sharing your vibration with them. Feel the resulting vibration rise in their vibration. It is important not to tell someone you are doing this for them or to take credit for any change in their behavior. If their vibration does permanently shift upwards, it's because they shifted. I have seen changes in people's behavior in positive ways after doing this, but I knew it was because they took the gift and used it.

Another fun way to do this for yourself is to find a person who you admire overall or in certain areas. For example, it could be the Dali Lama's level of peace or Oprah's business and financial success. Feel your own vibration, then intend to feel the celebrity's vibration in the area you want to focus on, and then try to match it.

You can also ask their higher self to help you by sharing their vibration with you. Complete the exercise by feeling grateful for the shift in your vibration.

We're All In this Together

We come from the same energy and we return to the same energy. When we help each other we help ourselves and vice versa. Life is set up so that we are blessed when we bless others. I know many of us have been taught differently and some people believe there is not enough for everyone, but as you work with some of these exercises and intend to shift your story, you will find that we can all be successful in life.

BONUS!

Sign up and receive your free audios and PDFs.

- See Yourself Through God's Eye's Audio
- Connect with Higher Selves Audio

dailyalchemy.com/personal-alchemy-book/

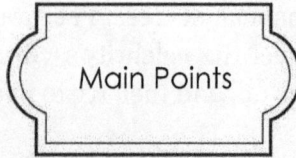

Main Points

- You are not the only energetic ingredient in your recipe.

- How you interact with other people's vibrations is also part of your personal alchemy.

- Others are drawn to you and your work based on the vibrations associated with you and your work.

- A higher vibration has much more power than a lower vibration.

- Seeing people as God sees them can shift how you experience them.

- Acts of love toward others raises your vibration and theirs.

- Sending out love or energy into the world can change others more than we realize.

- There is a gift in every perceived problem or flaw.

- We can raise vibrations by mixing two different vibrations.

- We are all interconnected; when we improve our own alchemy, we help improve everyone else's, too.

Chapter Five:

There's More than Me and You Here

I've already mentioned God in this book and I usually put in this disclaimer: you don't have to believe in God or use the term God if it makes you uncomfortable. In fact, if spiritual pursuits don't light you up, you can just skip this chapter. You've already learned enough to make lasting changes in your vibration.

However, for me, the spiritual connection is what really matters, what makes life worthwhile. When I feel the spiritual connection to everyone and everything, it brings me joy to know that God is part of everything – including me. Some of us may have grown up being presented with the concept of a stern and unloving God. If that was the case for you, choose a different term, such as Universe, Goddess, Spirit, or Pam Grout's term, the Field of Potentiality.

Why Connecting with Spirit Makes Everything Easier

H. Emilie Cady, the author of *Lessons in Truth*, said that as we grow more spiritually focused, we lose our personality and increase our individuality. Individuality comprises the traits you were created with that are the real you, but personality is the way you express yourself based on how you are vibrating right now. Personality is often based on trying to be who you think the people around you *want* you to be, or from vibrations you picked up early in life from family and friends that you may not even resonate with. When you choose to focus spiritually, you shift your vibration and the false personality begins to fall away. You express more of your true self. That's personal alchemy in action; it's what brings a change in who you are, and as a result, in how you experience life. We may not like people's personalities, but individuality is always truly beautiful.

Brother Lawrence, a Carmelite monk who lived in the 1600s, experienced this profoundly. He focused on loving God and practiced being in the presence of God so fully that he became very joyful. He was a monk assigned to kitchen and garbage duty long before running water, dishwashers, and other modern conveniences. It was hard and often smelly work, but he was so deeply immersed in God's love as he performed it that his work became a meditation that raised his vibration.

When the bells rang signaling chapel time, he loathed to stop his work and go pray because he felt closer to God while carrying out his duties. His letters were compiled in a book called *The Practice of the Presence of God*. You don't have to be a monk to benefit from his practice. He carried it out simply as he went about his day-to-day life, and you can, too. Just intend to feel God's presence with you as you do everything you do, and focus on it in your mind as often as you can. By doing this, you will feel the same joy Brother Lawrence did.

What Kind of Spiritual are We Talking About?

It doesn't really matter what your specific beliefs are. You can do these exercises whether you are Christian, Jewish, Muslim, Buddhist or even if you prescribe to no organized religion at all. I myself tend to agree with Pam Young, author of *The Joy of Being Disorganized*, who described herself as "Christmushindjewbud" once she came to believe that all religions had a level of oneness in them. A Unity church was where I began my spiritual journey, and the Unity School of Christianity still holds a special place in my heart. I also enjoy going to services in every faith, from Hindu ashrams and temples to Catholic Mass. Anywhere love is present I can find something worthwhile for my vibration. I go where my heart leads me – I hope you will too.

Even if you don't believe in God at all you can still get some benefit from connection with the vibrations of the natural world. The following exercises are to help you connect with a variety of different spiritual connections – not just to God, but to a lot of the different types of vibrations available on our planet. As always, choose the ones that resonate with you, and leave the rest.

Exercise 1: Explore Other Supportive Practices, Disciplines & Props

I don't think you *need* any outside thing to help us connect to spirit or to work on your personal alchemy, *but* it can be helpful in some cases. I used to use a pendulum to ask yes and no questions daily in my life. Now I never do. I check in with my gut and my feelings tell me yes or no. I've gotten to a level where I know how to tap into my own higher self and get answers from within.

I was never a big fan of muscle testing or kinesiology myself but some people swear by it. I also used to read my angel and other oracle cards daily. Now I only pull them when I feel I need some extra support, which is usually only every six months or so. The props I use now are mostly crystals and essential oils whose energies I resonate with or that hold the type of vibrations I desire to connect with. In time, I may not use any props at all or I may always enjoy them on some level.

Props are not bad at all as long as we realize we don't have to have them. We have the ability to connect within ourselves. It reminds me of when I started yoga and my guru said, 'You start where you are. At first, you might need blocks or rolls to help you hold the position; use them when you need them. In time you'll be strong enough you no longer need them, but some days you still might want to use them.' It is worth exploring whether or not you are drawn to any of these items or disciplines and, if you are, play with them and see if you get benefits from using them. Some might resonate so deeply you will practice them throughout your life and others might be good just to get you through a certain phase of growth.

Some of the props, practices and disciplines available to us are:

Pendulums: Used for yes or no questions. You can buy these on E-bay or other online sites. Most are made from metal, crystals or wood. They are very simple to use. You just carry them around with you for a day or two, maybe in your pocket and sleep with them under your pillow. Give them a chance to be charged with your energy. Once a few days have passed, you can hold the pendulum chain with your thumb and pointer finger. Ask the pendulum, what is yes, no, and unable to answer now. The normal responses are: clockwise for "yes", counterclockwise for "no" and back and forth for unable to answer now. It might be slightly different for you, so ask the pendulum to show you "yes", "no" and "needs more information." Then, you can use it to ask any yes or no question that you want some input on. This uses the same premise as muscle testing, that your subconscious mind will influence the pendulum to give you the answers that are true for you at that moment.

Angel cards or other oracle cards: You can get these from various sources. My favorites are Doreen Virtue's decks. Most cards come with a book that will explain how to do a reading for yourself and others. You can do detailed readings or just pull a card a day for a little guidance.

Essential oils: These oils are distilled to get to the purest essence and vibration of the plant, so they are great for helping shift your vibration. Different oils are good for different things. I am a big fan of essential oils and almost always have them diffusing in my house. I put on different oils for different needs, such as peppermint when I want energy or lavender when I want to relax. I also have many oils that are blended together to help create a certain mood.

Crystals: Crystals have strong vibrations and carrying them or meditating with them can help you shift your vibration. Certain crystals are tuned to help you work on certain areas of life. You can also learn healing techniques with crystals. There are many great websites and online courses to learn about crystals. My favorite place to get the scoop on crystals is at hibiscusmooncrystalacademy.com. You can also go to a store where you can pick up the crystals one at a time. Buy the ones that feel good to you and use your intuition to know when to carry certain crystals, or meditate with one based on how it feels to you.

Astrology: Astrology doesn't determine our fate as some people think; rather we are born at times that match our personality, vibration, and life path. Astrology can give you guidance to know yourself better and learn the best ways to act for your own personal growth. When you study astrology, choose someone who interprets it from a positive perspective like Kim Falconer and Jeanette Maw at www.goodvibeastrology.com or Rob Bresny at www.freewillastrology.com.

Traditional alchemy and astrology overlap, as many experiments are completed at different times or days based on what planet is ruling the sky, because different planets have different energy signatures or vibrations. The planets also correspond to different metals used in alchemical experiments. I have found that you don't have to check astrology for everything, because once you have lined up your vibration you just naturally do things at the perfect time. However, if you are doing practical alchemy or planning something big like your wedding date or launching a new business, you might want to consult the stars.

In my alchemical training, astrology is a necessary ingredient, so if you plan to delve deeper into practical alchemy, you will want to learn more about astrology as well. You can learn how to make your chart online for free at Astro.com and Good Vibe Astrology is my favorite place to learn to interpret your chart. Kim Falconer has many videos on her YouTube channel at https://www.youtube.com/user/Annadusa to walk you through the basics. Many alchemy books teach the basic astrology you will need to complete alchemical processes. It is a great way to learn more about yourself and how you might be vibrating.

Numerology: Numerology is the study of numbers. It uses the numbers in your birth date and those encoded in your name to give you more information about yourself. I was not really interested in it until I had a reading done by Janette Dalgliesh at sweetreliefcoaching.com. The information she gave me about myself was astounding. When I made the change in my professional name that she suggested, I sold an article to a magazine that had been rejected five times before.

Another aspect of numerology I find interesting is when you notice a number repeated often, such as 111 or 222, or any number that keeps showing up to you, you can look up the meaning behind that number and it may give you insight. You can find the meanings of many number combinations at spiritlibrary.com/doreen-virtue/number-sequences-from-the-angels.

Exercise 2: Call In Angels

This is an exercise I learned many years ago from Doreen Virtue. There are angels available to us for all of our needs. They love to be called upon. When you desire a mood, call on the angels to enhance or change it. I often call on the angels of laughter and good times during long, family car trips. I'll ask for angels of romance and love to be with me and my husband on our date nights. Angels aren't just for emergencies – I call on them daily, visualize them and feel the presence of their vibration.

Exercise 3: Give Love To A Plant

This exercise may surprise you, but you will probably be amazed by the strength of your love once you complete it. Consciously decide to give love to a plant you already have, or buy a small one and see what happens. When I did this experiment, we had two plants in our house that we had purchased at the same time; they were the same type of plant and were at about the same stage of dying. Yes, *dying*. In the past, I haven't always been the best at caring for plants, even though I love them. I decided to give love to one plant and ignore the other plant, except I would start watering both and giving them more sun. The results were amazing. Only three days after I stated my intention, the plant that was being ignored had shriveled up and was totally brown, but the plant I was sending love to had already sprouted three new stalks. Sadly, the other plant was beyond repair, but the other one continues to thrive. All I do is sit for a few minutes, think and say loving words to the plant, and picture it surrounded by white light... and it grows! Give it a try for yourself. You can use two plants to compare the difference like I did, or just focus on helping one plant blossom.

Exercise 4: Mother Earth Love

Gaia is the name given to Earth as a living organism, which we are all a part of. Whether or not you subscribe to the belief that our planet is alive and we are part of its being as some of the "cells" that make up her body, we are an important part of our planet. We impact the planet with our actions and our vibrations. Since our vibrational level impacts how we think and behave – and ultimately how we treat our planet – spending some time connecting with the planet we live on is wise. I sometimes lie on the grass in the summer and picture myself connecting to the earth and sending love over and throughout it until I can feel the whole planet vibrating with love. When it's not nice outside I do this in a chair, with my feet resting on the ground, and imagine the love energy going out through my feet and into the planet.

Many of us are concerned about the state of our planet and whether we are damaging it beyond repair with the pollution we are causing. The more people who send healing love to the planet, the healthier it will be. This love also creates a vibration that will help us receive ideas on the best way to heal our planet and to live on without damaging it. We can be healthy antibodies and not cancer cells for our planet – the choice is ours. I've found that when you give love to the planet, you receive its love in return... and Gaia has a very strong level of love.

Exercise 5: Feng Shui

Feng Shui is the ancient art of directing the energy in your home, other buildings and the outside environment. It teaches you to arrange your home and your possessions in such a way to best let energy flow, to create peace in your life. I find that this happens quite naturally for some of us – we know how to place things to mirror our lives, even when we don't know about Feng Shui.

When we want to change our thinking, making a change in our environment can help us shift our vibration. Our vibration permeates the places where we hangout, but those places also have their own vibrations that can be shifted by making simple changes to the environment. *Clear Your Clutter with Feng Shui* by Karen Kingston is one of my favorite guidebooks to basic Feng Shui. It's easy for westerners to follow and doesn't get complicated like lots of books do. There's no reason to go deep into the rules of Feng Shui unless it brings you joy. Here are just a few simple tips that I follow to make my house and office feel so much better:

1) *Get rid of clutter*. If you don't love it and need it, it goes. Clutter clogs up the energy of a space and signals the universe that you have a lack of consciousness. If you are afraid to let go of items you don't need, ask yourself why. Are you afraid you might need it someday? Do you not trust

that you will be able to have what you need when you need it? Karen Kingston's book and the Flylady's program of de-cluttering at www.flylady.net can help if you have difficulty letting go. If any object has a bad memory associated with it, get rid of it now! Even if you need it. Even if you used to love it. If it makes you think of something unpleasant, it goes. Get a new one of whatever it is that makes you smile. Life is too short to look at something every day that makes you sad.

2) *Arrange items in your house in a way that feels good to you and allows people to move easily though spaces.* Don't block doorways or walkways.

3) *Look up the Bagua or Feng Shui energy map online and place a few items in specific areas of your house that you would like to improve.* The Bagua areas are: family & health, wealth, relationships, children and creativity, helpful people and travel, fame and reputation, knowledge, and good fortune.

Find the part of your house or rooms that correspond to an area on the map you would like to improve, and then add something meaningful to that area. For example, if you are looking for more love, find an object that symbolizes love to you, like a rose quartz or a picture of a happy couple, and place it in that area.

Just those few simple steps are enough to raise the vibration in your house.

Exercise 6: Vibration Mixology with the Spirit World

This exercise is done in the same way you did between yourself and other people, except you do the same process with angels, God, crystals and essential oils. You can choose to mix your vibration with the vibration of an essential oil or crystal that has a particular pull for you or is helpful in an area you want to improve in your life. You can also choose to focus on the angels you called in one of the previous exercises, or a specific archangel. You could also focus on a place in nature such as the Grand Canyon, a beautiful waterfall, or even a certain planet, the sun, or the moon. You might choose to focus on God's vibration, but for some this may feel too intense or unreachable.

Focus on feeling your own vibration in your left hand, then focus on feeling the vibration of what you want to experience in your right hand. Now place your right hand on top of your left and let the vibrations combine into a single new vibration, and allow it to spread throughout your body. Always do this with the intention that you will end up feeling more joyful and with a higher vibration than you started.

Exercise 7: Surrender

Sometimes, there's nothing else to do but just be. Be who you are, soaking up everything that's good in your life, everything that's wonderful and perfect. But if you're in a place where you can't do anything and you feel like crap, it's time to hand it all over to God or whatever spiritual connection works for you.

I do this in a yoga position called child's pose. Some people prostate themselves, and some just sit in chair with their eyes closed – what matters is your intent. Open your heart to God and acknowledge that you are done. You can't do any more, and you're handing things over for a while. This doesn't mean you give up on your dreams or on having a happy life – it just means you need a break from trying.

There comes a time when we need to just let go and be, and let God love us and help us. Tell God whatever is going on that sucks and ask for help to shift your vibration for you. You've made movement, you've taken inspired action, now you just need spirit to take over for a while and let it help everything gel.

When you do this physical act of surrendering, stay there until you feel a shift in your vibration that signals you have indeed let go. Any small feeling of relief means success.

Now take the time you need; do as little as possible, give yourself a break. Don't be social unless you want to. Don't do any more work than the bare minimum and take a total work break if you can. Know that God is there working behind the scenes. You are going to feel so much better and ready to create in the world again soon.

BONUS!

Sign up and receive your free PDF.

- Angel Assignment Form

dailyalchemy.com/personal-alchemy-book/

Main Points

- For many it's important to include the spiritual world in our personal alchemy practice.

- Individuality is who we are; personality is how we're expressing our vibration now.

- Focusing on spiritual growth helps us naturally begin to express more of our individuality and less of a "fake" personality.

- Props to shift our vibration are fine to use, as long as we enjoy them and don't rely solely upon them.

- Sending love to plants can show you how strong the power of love is.

- We are all part of the being that is Earth.

- Getting rid of clutter and arranging your house can raise the vibration of your environment, and in turn your own vibration will shift.

- We can raise our vibration by mixing in the vibrations of the natural and spirit world.

- Sometimes that best step to take is to surrender to God.

Chapter Six:

Balance - The Right Mix of Ingredients

Now that you've practiced some of the different ways you can affect your personal alchemy, the last step is to put it all together in the way that makes the most sense for you. The most important ingredients are you and your personal alchemy, so start there first. Then add in other people, objects, angels and God in whatever mix feels right to you. Remember, you are unique and the results you achieve when working with personal alchemy and the law of attraction will also be unique.

If my life begins to feel stagnant, I will look to see what area I am neglecting. Most of us tend to neglect ourselves. Once we have been trained to love ourselves, we might find that we need to eventually focus on giving to others. I know giving gifts or sharing time with others causes a big shift and can increase not only my joy, but also the positive experiences that occur in my life.

Remember, you don't need to make yourself into a better person than you are now. You just want to express more and more of your natural vibrations and your own true individuality. You are a precious gift to the world and the more you believe this, the more it will become your reality.

The two most important exercises in this book are the first and the last – your statement of being and surrender. Deciding your purpose on this planet and crafting your statement of being gives direction to everything you do. You always know what the big picture is. Yes, I want to be an author and I want to publish my books, but knowing that I want to promote love in the world is going to influence how I go about achieving my goals and if I need to change them. All of my goals are designed with my overall statement of being in mind. If my goals are not in alignment with my purpose, then I'm not likely to have much success or feel as blissful as I could.

When your goals are in line and you are doing everything in a way that feels right to you, but negativity has snuck into your thoughts, surrender is the strongest action. It's not weak to give yourself a break and lean on God and the universe for a while. Just letting go and following the flow of life can bring magic into your existence. Shifting your intentions and how you feel about personal alchemy will create massive changes in your life, whether or not you add law of attraction techniques to these exercises. Improving how you feel about yourself and revealing more of your true self will change your life.

One Woman's Successful Recipe for Using Personal Alchemy and the Law of Attraction

Helene Hadsell has been called the woman who wins every contest. She has won over 5,000 – including numerous trips and a house! She released an audio program and e-book a few years back that I purchased.

Helene shares the step-by-step process that she uses to win prizes. Even though I followed her recommendations, I didn't have her level of success. I did win several contests, but the method that worked for me was different from the one she proposed. Her method mostly revolved around the law of attraction and visualizing herself experiencing the feeling of winning. When I followed her steps and entered contests, I won nothing. However, in her story she talks about learning the Silva Method and other meditation techniques early in her life, and that this shifted her vibration. Plus, she was a naturally generous person, who helped friends, family and even strangers win contests, as well. This inspired me.

Ultimately, the technique I used to win contests was forgetting about the prize and focusing on being of service. Once, I spent a day volunteering at my daughter's school preparing for the school carnival. I practiced being in the presence of God like Brother Lawrence and tried to be in the moment enjoying doing all the helpful tasks I could. At the end of the day, I enjoyed the carnival with my children. I was so surprised when I won the large basket in the raffle worth $500 and my daughter won an iPod for selling me the tickets. I only bought the tickets to help the school and not to try to win. So Helene and I had two different winning techniques. She was definitely more successful than I was at winning contests, however, and that was likely because she had both the law of attraction and personal alchemy on her side.

Whether you decide to add some law of attraction techniques in with your practice of personal alchemy or not, you have the keys to creating a happy life and I'm sure you can create just the right recipe to suit your own personal tastes.

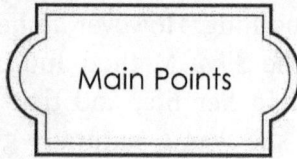

Main Points

- You are unique and that's wonderful news.

- Start with yourself and then add in others.

- If life isn't shifting positively, look at your balance.

- Focus on your statement of being.

- Allow yourself to surrender if you need to.

- You can create a happy life by focusing on your personal alchemy and adding in other law of attraction techniques if you desire.

Suggested Reading

E-squared: 9 Do-It-Yourself Energy Experiments that Prove Your Thoughts Create Your Reality by Pam Grout has so many wonderful experiments you can do to convince yourself that the law of attraction and God's love for you are real.

The Art of Self Love is an e-book by Jeannette Maw that will lead you to even deeper levels of self-love, which is always a good thing. You can find it on www.goodvibeblog.com

Power vs. Force by David Hawkins is great to learn more about the vibrational nature of our universe.

Clear Your Clutter with Feng Shui by Karen Kingston is my go-to book for simple Feng Shui techniques.

The Practice of the Presence of God by Brother Lawrence is one of my favorite books about changing your life by focusing on God's love constantly. It is a series of letters written in the 1600s by Brother Lawrence and not a traditional self-help book, but his words are gifts to the world.

Hibiscus Moon at hybiscusmooncrystalacademy.com is my favorite source for information on crystals in a fun and funky language.

The Complete Idiot's Guide to Alchemy by Dennis William Hauck is a great source if you want to dive deeper into traditional alchemy.

Kim Falconer at the Eleventh House (kimfalconer.wordpress.com) will teach you that astrology didn't create your fate but that the stars lined up with who you are to give you a map of your unique soul. Looking at it from that perspective can give you lots of insight about your individuality.

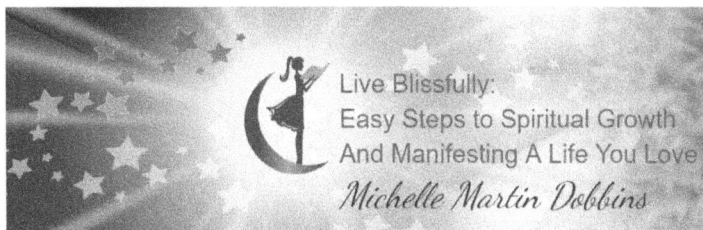

Live Blissfully:
Easy Steps to Spiritual Growth
And Manifesting A Life You Love
Michelle Martin Dobbins

Freebies Only for the Readers of Personal Alchemy

Thank you for purchasing my book, *Personal Alchemy*, and taking the time to read it!

May you have found some tips that help you find more joy and love in your life.

Sign up to receive all the free audios and forms mentioned in the book.

- What is the Difference Between Alchemy and Law of Attraction?
- See Yourself Through God's Eye's Audio
- Connect with Higher Selves Audio
- Vibe-Mixology Intro Audio
- Daily Love List Planning Form & Audio
- Angel Assignment Form

dailyalchemy.com/personal-alchemy-book/

Acknowledgments

I could never have completed this book without many wonderful people supporting me.

First, I want to thank my parents, Velma and Merel Martin, for loving me and allowing me to be myself, even though my own personality is quite different from theirs. It's so much easier to follow your own path when you have that vital support from birth.

I've met so many amazing people who have helped me so much. I met Reverend Dick Andrews at Christ Church Unity in Augusta, Georgia in 1992 and he introduced me to a whole new way of thinking, and saved my life in many ways. He performed the marriage ceremony for my husband and I about a year before he passed away. I'll never forget him and the changes he helped me create in my world. He truly was a master at personal alchemy. He created so much love and miracles in his life.

Jeannette Maw was my first coach and seven years later, she's still my coach and gives me the best advice. Pam Grout has inspired me and reminded me that rejection is part of being a writer. Kim Falconer and Janette Dalgliesh have helped me with their respective astrology and numerology skills and created a path with their writing success that I hope to emulate.

I've also met many wonderful people through my blog, Facebook, and Twitter. Thanks to all of you who have encouraged me and let me know that my words touched you.

My husband, David Dobbins, has always encouraged me to follow my dreams and has tolerated lots of nights listening to me typing while he tries to sleep. Serenity, my oldest daughter, gives me wonderful critiques and encouragement. Her younger siblings, Kadin, Kali and Violet are the best fans any writer could have. They love to tell people that their mommy is a writer and that fortifies me to not give up. I am truly very blessed by all the wonderful people in my life who support me. Thank you all.

~Michelle Martin Dobbins

About The Author

Michelle Martin Dobbins is an author, spiritual alchemist & reiki master who shares true stories of magic, creation and love in everyday life at dailyalchemy.com. She adores reading, writing, meditating, homeschooling her four children and supporting people to transform their lives using love and joy... Oh, and chocolate. Lots of chocolate.

Connect with Michelle:

- MichelleDobbinsAuthor
- @MichelleDobbins
- MichelleMartinDobbins
- MichelleMartinDobbins
- DMDobbins98